CHURCH AND THE MODERN WOMAN

Olu and Vicki David

Revealed Word Publishers

Unless otherwise indicated, all scripture quotations are taken from the King James Version of the Bible.

The Church and The Modern Woman

ISBN:9798850339043

Copyright © 2023 by Olu and Vicki David

Published in Canada by:
Revealed Word Publishers

6&7-377 MacKenzie Avenue,
Ajax, ON L1S 2G2

Tel:+1-905 686 1544
Text/Whatsapp: +1-905 767 0925
 +1-905 242 7818

Email:info@relationsnet.org

Website: www.relationsnet.org
           www.rhomiministries.com

All rights reserved under International Copyright. Contents and/or cover may not be reproduced in whole or in part in any form without the express permission of the publisher.

CONTENTS

Preface — 4

1. The oppression of women — 12
2. The response of the feminist movement — 17
3. The backlash of the feminist movement — 31
4. Who is a woman according to the scripture? — 43
5. The feminine woman and her man — 71

READ PRAYERFULLY

I want to encourage you to read this book prayerfully. This book will only make sense to you if you value God's word, because it is full of stronghold-breaking and table-shaking truths. You may also need to read it many times over.

PREFACE

It is imperative that I give a bit of background information on the how, why and importance of this book. I have been married for 35 years to a woman who has been my best friend for more than 40 years. We have a good marriage and many couples look up to us as the ideal couple. We have mentored and ministered to hundreds over the years and continue to do so. My wife has said frequently in conferences as she ministers around the world that we have a peaceful home and a good marriage, and that is absolutely correct. We have had our moments of disagreements and trials but it has never gotten out of hand, neither have we ever had to involve a third party to resolve a situation.

A few years ago, I took some time off to pray and fast, seeking the Lord for the ministry and what He would have me do next.
On the third day of my dry fast just before I took a cup of juice to ease the fast the Lord spoke to me and said, "Go

and take care of your wife." I was a little surprised at this instruction because first, I came to hear God about the next level of my ministry assignment and secondly I was already taking care of my wife (or so I thought).
But God was about to show me that beyond spiritual covering, and physical and financial care there was a whole lot more I needed to learn.

As I sat at His feet to study, search, research, meditate and understand, He showed me the gender war that has been raging for decades and which in recent years has heated up to another level among the younger generation; the war that has brought toxic femininity and toxic masculinity to the forefront.
He showed me the level of all manner of abuse, put downs and shut downs that women have had to endure in many marriages; while in some cases the husbands are oblivious of what they are doing to their wives, some know, but the love of self, power and control blinds them from doing the right thing.

He showed me what real Connection, Communication and Emotional management in marriage is all about. Then he showed me areas where I had failed in attending to, caring for and connecting my wife.
I saw that although my wife and I were together, our connection in some areas had widened over the years and we didn't even know it. So I broke my fast, received grace and humbly returned home to my wife. On getting home I apologized to her for my lack of care and controlling behavior and told her what God had instructed me.

She takes it from here in her own words.

"My husband returned home from his usual fasting and praying for the ministry and He told me that God's instruction for the next level of ministry was for Him to take care of me. Sincerely, that didn't make sense to me and I kind of chuckled and asked him, "What do you mean take care of me?" I said, "Looking around, I am yet to see a marriage doing better. You pray for me, you wait on the Lord to receive messages for me that I take around the world. You have always been a responsible husband and father, you spend and you're spent, you have never raised your hand to hit me neither has there been any incidence of sexual infidelity. I see you trusting God and working very hard to financially support the conferences I host around the world so that I'm not pressured to call for offerings that God has not asked me to take, (not that it's wrong to take up offerings), I don't understand'.

Then he said, "Some of the ways I've been treating you is not right. I want to apologize for taking steps that impact the home and family without you fully being on board and controlling how most things are done. I am sorry for the way I shut you down sometimes, my impatience, jumping into your sentences before you're done talking and taking over the conversation, not giving you adequate respect in vital decision making, not taking time to be gentle with you….all such behavior is not right."

As he spoke I felt healed, I felt better and my heart in a strange way just warmed towards him. I felt his love and gave him a warm hug.

He had not made any physical changes to the way he says and does things, but by just acknowledging and apologizing for these behaviors, my soul was refreshed. I had protested about these things many times before, but when there was no change after so many years I stopped talking.

What I didn't know was that though I had stopped talking, and the home and ministry was still running smoothly and peacefully, a part of our connection had been negatively impacted.

The next day for the first time my husband made me breakfast before I woke up and continued to do so till I told him we'll do it together. He took over the blending of my smoothies till date (a variety of them that I make for different purposes and taste), while I hang around him and talk. Although we have people around us who can do these things he chose to do them.

He took me shopping for some fine/elegant clothing and jewelry to wear on a regular basis. These are clothes I only shop for when I'm going to conferences, not because we couldn't afford it but because it wasn't really our priority. For the first time he drove me to a spa to have a manicure and pedicure and has continued to do so till date.

Making sure I had a vehicle of my choice has always been his priority but this time he insisted on getting me a new series Mercedes Benz coupe that was just for me not the seven seat SUV to "carry" people that I was clamoring for.

In his words, "Mama you have been sacrificing

for everybody: church, ministry and family, and that's a good thing, but now it's time to take care of yourself and enjoy the life that God gave you." It was then it dawned on me how much both of us had put aside my personal needs for others and for the ministry, although by the grace of God I could have spoiled myself as often as I wanted.

Importantly I saw him working hard not to cut me off mid-sentence, waiting patiently for me while I get dressed if we are going out together, taking time to listen to, understand and respect my opinions even when it is different from his; and making sure I was fully on board in the decision making at home and in the ministry.

In addition to all this he took time to call me beautiful and attractive. Daily he told me, "I love you my dear", followed by a kiss. During the summer, he found somewhere to take me to every weekend.

The more gentle, caring and attentive he became, the more I opened up to him. In the process I was able to open up to him about the impact menopause and advancing in age had brought to my body which had in turn negatively impacted my physiological and emotional well-being. I couldn't talk about it because I just wasn't used to talking like that. They were little things but they had become very big in my mind and I became a little nonchalant about my looks and dressing.

His care revived me. Unknown to me this was the medication I needed. Being loved genuinely, affirmed often, cared for, encouraged and complimented was the cure I needed. Looking back now this was Jesus loving me back to health through my husband.

Wow! This level of involvement, care and attention for my personal needs made me glow from within and it was evident to all around me
I found back my zeal and passion. I now began to look forward to the next twenty years of ministry, if Christ has not returned or called me home.

I was blown away, and the level of our connection, communication and intimacy took a new dimension. The switch was beautiful to behold and it took me a while to get used to this new life, but I have since done away with my traditional mindset and have adjusted to the fact that this is the way it should be in the order of Divine Concept. Honor for Honor, Respect for Respect and Love for my Submission."

Vicki Olu-David

As I continued to obey the Lord in my home I saw the need for the church of God to understand that:
1. Men have been unduly empowered by the traditional concept of marriage.
2. It takes grace and strength to relinquish the total hold on power and share it.
3. Nothing helps a man to be a better husband than Christ.
4. The freedom women are fighting for are all found in the love of a man in Christ.

This led to the birth of Relationship Network-a ministry to married couples and mature singles.

THE NEGLECTED PILLAR

The LORD Jesus warned the religious leaders of His days about neglecting the most important, and said we don't have to neglect one for the other"…… But you have neglected the more important matters of the law – justice, mercy and faithfulness. You should have practiced the latter, without neglecting the former." Mathew.23:23

In every building project, there are certain structural elements that must be in place in order to erect a strong structural building. As such is the divine concept of marriage and family.
Neglecting of family and marital relationship concepts as one of the main pillars of church building is ceding advantage to the enemy.

All churches must do every other outreach plus relationship network. One family under attack in any church is one too many and also too toxic for the health of the corporate family. Many shining stars, preachers and leaders have been taken down and others are just one major relationship attack/strike away.

Marital relationship breakdowns must not be allowed to fester or gain any ground in the churches of Christ and lack of strong family network is denying those under attack from getting the structural support they need.

Sneak attacks on marital unions and sexual corruption are top on the list of satanic agenda manifesting in these times. Hijacking divine marital relationship idea, corrupting family concept through/by culture, tradition and wrong psychology has become the tool of the powers of darkness to waste, delay and derail destinies today. Children and Youth are often the ultimate targets of such relationship failures. Studies have revealed that many youths are on anti-depressant medication.

Marital union is heavenly. The joining of a man to a woman to form one is a mystery of divinity.
The Lord Jesus is a husband and a groom waiting for His bride. There is one and only glorious wedding which no one can ever gate-crash and it is taking place in heaven. God functions in a family concept as a Father with a family in heaven and on earth. We are first sons and daughters before any other ministry title or function.

Marriage after divine order is absolutely adorable and super healthy for raising homes, societies/communities and nations. Who do you think is against this and would oppose this? Why do you think the anti-Christ's spirit and his crowd are doing everything they can to hijack, change, adulterate and proffer alternatives to divine concept of marriage and family? Because it is God's idea and agenda and the anti-Christ's mission is basically to oppose all that is of God.
"Who opposeth and exalteth himself
above all that is called God, or that is worshipped; so that he as God sitteth in the temple of God, shewing himself that he is God." 2 Thess. 2:4 KJV.

Wholesome relationships are established on the pillars of connection, communication and emotional management and this is what this book is all about.

OLU DAVID

1

"Rather than attend to their cries, the oppression and regression was perpetuated by the doctrine of, "God hates divorce", "wife submit to your own husband" etc.
And often rebuffed by her own parents and peers, she was asked to endure, because marriage is a learning center for women and she has to tolerate it."

THE OPPRESSION OF WOMEN

THE PROPHECY OF THE END TIMES:

"AND IN that day seven women shall take hold of one man, saying, We will eat our own bread and provide our own apparel; only let us be called by your name to take away our reproach [of being unmarried]."….. Isaiah 4:1 AMPC"

"Therefore will I give their wives to others and their fields to those who gain possession of them; for everyone, from the least even to the greatest, is given to covetousness (is greedy for unjust gain); from the prophet even to the priest, everyone deals falsely."….Jer.8:10

The prophecy of Isaiah above is already on the verge of becoming today's reality. Many men are tuning off from tying the knot in marriage for some of the reasons enumerated below and many modern women today are getting used to cheating on their husbands as a norm, exploiting the over fantasied sexual world out there.

By today's statistics men aren't getting married as they used to.

Only around 40% of marriage age men are married today for reasons ranging from socio-economic to marriage instability, to lopsided government interference and more importantly the sting of the rising feminist movement! The percentage of women cheating today are almost at par with that of men!

Divorce rates are sky-high: 45% of marriages end in divorce, and women initiate 80% of them and 90% of the women are college graduates according to studies.
Men are not marrying because, the cost and dangers of divorce outweighs the benefits of marriage.
It is becoming extremely hard for modern women to find dates even online today because of the ever rising toxic masculinity in response to toxic femininity.

WOMEN OPPRESSION IN HISTORY

Misogyny is hatred of, contempt for, or prejudice against women. It is a form of sexism that is used to keep women at a lower social status than men, thus maintaining the social roles of patriarchy. (Wikipedia.org)
Oppression is an abuse of personal authority and the use of privileges to deny others their equitable rights. The injustice of oppression can keep someone permanently at

the bottom of the social ladder. The psychological effect of mental oppression especially with oppressive ideas can leave the victim with a depressive mental burden.

Women have been unjustly held back from achieving full equality for much of human history in many societies around the world.
Feminist theorists of the 1960s and 1970s looked for new ways to analyze this oppression, often concluding that there were both overt and insidious forces in society that oppressed women.
These feminists also drew on the work of earlier authors who had analyzed the oppression of women,
including Simone de Beauvoir in "The Second Sex"
and Mary Wollstonecraft in "A Vindication of the Rights of Woman".

WOMEN'S OPPRESSION EVERYWHERE

Women's oppression by men in European, Middle Eastern, and African cultures are common features of early centuries. In almost all societies, women's political, educational, social and legal rights were firmly denied.

The practice of wives, consorts, or retainers following a husband, lord, or ruler in death has been attested at many points in history and in every region of the world, including Asia, Africa, Europe, and the Americas. In the Confucian cultures of China and Korea and the Hindu cultures of India and Indonesia. (The Oxford Encyclopedia Women in World History)

There are cultures today where women are not allowed in public spheres.

SEXUAL VIOLENCE

Women everywhere have reported cases of rape, forced intercourse by male authority figures in all areas of society from school to churches to workplace and nothing could be more cruel than this in the grade of oppression.
Sexual violence and other forms of violence can create psychological trauma, and make it more difficult for victimized women to experience autonomy, choice, respect, and safety.

RELIGIONS AND CULTURAL CULPABILITY

In many cultures and religions, reproductive functions such as childbirth and menstruation, sometimes breastfeeding and pregnancy are seen as disgusting. Thus, in these cultures, women are often required to cover their bodies and faces.

Women are also treated either like children or like property in many cultures and religions. For example, the punishment for rape in some culture is that the rapist's wife is given over to the rape victim's husband or father to rape as he wishes, as revenge. Horrible!!

Or a woman who is involved in adultery or other sex acts outside monogamous marriage is punished more severely than the man who is involved, and a woman's word about rape is not taken as seriously as a man's word about being robbed would be. Women generally

live their lives with the status of somehow lesser than men permitted by culture and religion.
An example is the woman caught in adultery in the Bible. She was about to be stoned to death but where was the man she was caught with?

THE CRY FOR DELIVERANCE

Women in the early part of this century and up to the sixties began to cry for freedom from abuse and neglect in the hands of men. They organized and marched for equality with men, power sharing, financial and sexual freedom and these cries were largely ignored by the church.
Rather than attend to their cries, the oppression and regression was perpetuated by the doctrine of, "God hates divorce", "wife submit to your own husband" etc.

And often rebuffed by her own parents and peers, she was asked to endure, because marriage is a learning center for women and she has to tolerate it.
For the fear of losing opportunities, job, and status, and for the risk of cultural, religious and societal rejection, many women remained in those marriages, crying in silence up till today.

2

*"Traditional marriage is considered an avenue to foster male superiority and dominance over the female.
It is seen as a center of oppression and gender slavery for women in 7 major areas:"*

THE RESPONSE OF THE FEMINIST MOVEMENT

ADVENT OF THE FEMINIST MOVEMENT

According to the Feminist, the Feminist movement is a crusade to achieve full gender equality in law and in practice.
It's about respecting diverse women's experiences, identities, knowledge and strengths, and striving to empower all women to realize their full rights. It's about levelling the ground between genders, and ensuring that diverse women and girls have the same opportunities in life.
"Most feminists agree on five basic principles—working to increase equality, expanding human choice, eliminating gender stratification, ending sexual violence, and promoting sexual freedom."(Feminist Theory Overview, Beliefs & Types - Study.com)

The movement to grant women suffrage in the 19th and

20th centuries metamorphosed into the second wave of 1963 and then to the third wave of 1985 and into the fourth of 2012 and now gradually into the current state of modern women.

TRADITIONAL MARRIAGE IN THE VIEW OF THE FEMINIST MOVEMENT

In the feminist's definition, marriage is, in short, considered an 'intimate colonization' (Hagan, 1993). In feminist theory, wives are seen as subordinate, economically dependent and deferent (Johnson, 1988). In most if not all countries, women continue to have major responsibility for household and caring duties. (Van Every, 1995)
It is considered the chief vehicle for the perpetuation of the oppression of women; it is through the role of wife that the subjugation of women is maintained. It is believed that most women contrary to public facade are entangled in their marriages, suffering and crying for deliverance from their husband's oppression.

Traditional marriage is considered an avenue to foster male superiority and dominance over the female.
It is seen as a center of oppression and gender slavery for women in **7 major areas:**

A. **SEXUAL SUBJUGATION:** In most cultures, the traditional man often sees his wife as his sexual gratification object. She is bought to satisfy his sexual needs at all times whether she likes it or not. Men using the rules of traditional marriage subdued her sexuality.

Genital mutilation was introduced to kill her sexual pleasure.

She is seen and called promiscuous and shamed for wanting or liking sexual pleasure. She gets shamed for being sexually expressive.

She was told that she was created to satisfy a man's sexual need. That she doesn't need to enjoy sex but the man does and she just can't deny him even when she is not in the mood or is hurtful.

Below is a list of the kind of sexual subjugation some women go through in many traditional marriages.

1. He decides when sexual intimacy happens and ends.

2. Sexual fulfilment or pleasure are his monopoly.

3. He disregards her sexual needs or thoughts.

4. Orgasmic experience is also monopolized by him.

5. Her boundaries are hardly respected in the bedroom.

6. She feels constantly pressured and manipulated sexually.

7. He hardly checks in with her to know how she is feeling during intimacy.

B. **LACK OF FREEDOM.** Monitoring, questioning and limiting a woman's freedom in traditional marriages is often considered as normal but what is mostly ignored are the insecurities especially the emotional and physical insecurities that most men go into marriage with. The suspicions, lack of trust, display of negative ownership and overly possessive toxic masculinity often turn many traditional marriages into a prison home for many women.

Here are some of the things some men under traditional marital concept find okay to do to their wives.

1. He controls her movements, expressions, other relationships; and how she behaves,
dresses, and where she goes or who she sees.

2. He denies her access to necessary care and information just to manipulate her to "behave" accordingly.

3. He questions her judgments, thoughts and feelings and sometimes ridicule her ideas.

C. **ABUSE:** Domestic abuse, also called "domestic violence", can be defined as a pattern of behavior in any relationship that is used to gain or maintain power and control over a partner.
Below are various forms of abusive behavior that a man can subject his wife to:

1. **Emotional control**: He is Hyper-Critical of her thoughts, statements and actions, he ignores her

boundaries at will, he treats her like his bought property, heavily possessive, jealous and controlling and very dismissive of her feelings.
2. **Financial Control**: Using the family income, he manipulates and exerts control over her desires, actions and responses to get what he wants while leaving her to beg for hers.
3. **Physical:** Using physical force or threats of bodily harm, he manipulates her to get a response or an action from her.
4. **Sexual Control**: He sees and treats her as his sexual toy to satisfy his sexual gratification and she must not disappoint.
5. **Psychological/Verbal**: He messes with her mind, calls her horrible names to bend her will and make her conform to his bidding.

D. **NEGLECT:** There are many ways that many women get neglected in their marriages but the most damaging of them all is living with a man who is emotionally unavailable. Emotional neglect can cause a woman to be desensitized to her own femininity and consequently begin to develop and function from her resident masculinity. Women being emotional beings must be dialogued with through her feelings, and deliberately ignoring or not being in tune with her feelings will damage that womanhood within her. She will soon become stoic and start to respond or feel like a man. Here are some of the ways many men neglect the feelings of their women.

1. He denies her the necessary affection and care.

2. He avoids or shuts down conversations that are important to her.

3. He dictates the way he wants to love her and not the way she wants to be loved.

4. He puts her in a place where she finds it embarrassing to express her basic emotional needs to him.

5. He dismisses her feelings and needs while prioritizing his over hers.

E. INEQUALITY: Inequality often stems from the feeling of entitlement or superiority complex. The traditional marital concept confer on the male partner an undue superiority complex. Many men are like semi-gods in their home with absolute power and authority. She was made to marry him to worship him.

1. The responsibility of cleaning or tidying up is piled on her. She is often not better than an elevated home slave.

2. She does all the housework in most homes.

3. In most homes she solely takes care of raising the children.

F. LACK OF POWER AND DECISION SHARING:

The traditional marital concept confers on husbands the sole power and responsibility of making all destiny decisions about the family. This is absolutely not reflected in the way God by visitation, spoke to and instructed the mothers first concerning major biblical destinies in the scripture such as Jacob, Samson, Jesus, etc. Why would God speak to them first before their husbands?

Below is a list of some of the ways women can lose all power in family decision making:

1. He is often the one to decide where to go, sit, walk, sleep, live and what to eat, and who to do them with.

2. He alone has the final say on all major destiny choices that affects the family.

3. He alone decides how the family finances are handled.

4. He alone decides how the family spend their free time.

5. She has to ask him for permission in all things but he is not expected to do the same.

G. FINANCIAL DEPRIVATION:

Financial bullying tends to be covert, starting with little complaints about the high grocery bills or asking how much her dress costs.

As the relationship progresses, it escalates into

more serious behavior like limiting her spending, to giving her an allowance, to setting time and date of when and where she can get her own stuff, but somehow he is above the same rule.

Exerting financial control over a woman can lead to harmful financial deprivation which is mostly responsible for why today's modern women want their own money. A man in the name of traditional marriage can make his wife financially dependent, limit her ability to work, limit and control her spending desire/limit or even totally deny her access to the family funds unless she is "well behaved"

Below are some of the ways that women suffer financial deprivation in traditional marriages:

1. **Limited access to family funds:** Controlling access to funds can be extremely humiliating for a woman who knows she can work and make her own money. Traditional marriages in many cultures grants the husbands the sole control of the family funds and often times the personal needs of the wives if not totally neglected are at the bottom of the list.

2. **Spending control:** Most women under financial deprivation often resort to spending and hiding because her husband cannot resist the temptation of monitoring her spending.
Accessing online purchases/banking records and in-store purchases, can be an intense

manipulative behavior which is often responsible for triggering defensiveness, resentment and silent anger in many women in traditional marriages.

3. **Cheated on financially:** Financial cheating is very common in most traditional marriages where the husbands somehow feel no remorse spending family funds on extra-marital affairs while leaving their wives pleading and begging for grocery allowance. Some men will even swear that they have not been paid!

THE TRADITIONAL VS DIVINE CONCEPT IN MARRIAGE

"And the Lord God said, It is not good that the man should be alone; I will make him an help meet for him." Gen.2:18

Marriage concept, the idea of a man and a woman joined by God was originally a divine vision and established for the following reasons:
1. Mutual Friendship and Companionship.
2. Mutual Sexual Pleasure
3. Raising a Godly Family
4. Fulfillment of Life Assignments and Purpose

The wedding day is the most beautiful day every woman looks forward to. It is her day of joy and honor. She can't wait to throw the bouquet; looking forward to care, settlement, covering, protection, provision, etc., in the hand of the man she would call her husband.

Marriage is designed to be a haven of joy, harmony, fulfillment, peace and health, where everything godly and godliness is possible.

"And Adam said, this is now bone of my bones, and flesh of my flesh: she shall be called Woman, because she was taken out of Man. Therefore shall a man leave his father and his mother, and shall cleave unto his wife: and they shall be one flesh. And they were both naked, the man and his wife, and were not ashamed." Genesis 2:23-25

Adam woke up to the bone of his bones, flesh of his flesh. He saw a feminine man and called her woman. She is a refined product of the raw material in the man. Her root is in the man (1Cor 11:9)
From the very day Adam said, bone of my bone and flesh of my flesh, is the day that what we call marriage today began in history. A male plus female equals a man and that is simply beautiful.

But what do we have today? Why does the number of men and women seeking to tie the knot keep declining? It is like both men and women are saying, it is better to be alone than to be married.
So many marriages have become a theater where a lot of women go to suffer, a house of pain, filled with cycles of regret. Many women can't wait to get out of marriages they entered in joyfully.

From the day she said "I DO", her value, joy, beauty and health begins to slowly fade away under stressful marital conditions and situations.

Her husband has suddenly become her punisher, tormentor, terror, and antagonist. To many modern women today marriage is like a scam, an illusion, fairy tale, fantasy world that women are being deceived to fall for. She is not less to the man, neither is she dumb, subservient, undeserving, unintelligent and valueless just because she is a woman, and this she knows.

Likewise so many men don't want to touch marriage today. To them, it is considered a trap or slavery. It is like a place where men go to relinquish their man power, to work and work, pay and pay, to provide and protect and eventually get drained or destroyed by the divorce laws which is seen by men as heavily skewed in women's favor.

So many men who enter into marriage looking for support, rest, respect and regular sex become disappointed when faced with the emotional turmoil, mind games, fights, entanglement, and incessant complaints from their wives.

Listening to stories, experiences, statistics and lots of marriage counselors and relationship coaches these days on how to make marriage better; how tough and rough the journey can be; how difficult it is to maintain or remain in it; how you have to work so hard to hold it; how no marriage is perfect; how it is the only institution you are presented with a certificate before the exams; how it is not a business of happiness etc. it is like conditioning one's mind to accept or to cope with something that is not really good for one. It's like it is failing everywhere! Would a good God who said it is not good to be alone then give us what is not good for us? Why are traditional marriages really failing in droves?

Long before Christ came, marriage has been hijacked by the spirits/forces that created and ran the culture of men, and they established marital rituals/rites which vary from culture to culture in a satanic quest to adulterate, contaminate and deform divine agenda and purpose.
And because of the conflict between the serpent and the woman, and the curse on Eve and the daughters of men (Gen.4:15), the powers and principalities of darkness that oppose God's agenda on earth started traditional marriage in deviance to Divine order by injecting rituals and rules that establishes male dominance and superiority over their female partner knowing this is not divine order.

In traditional marriages, male superiority complexes are engrained in the mentality of many husbands making them think that marriage makes them better than their wives or more privileged and deserving.
Gender superiority, shaming and dominance are completely man-made and was injected into the marriage idea from God, to create the traditional concept.
And the church for years have ignorantly adopted this traditional concept as the order of marriage and the two cannot be further apart.

Traditional marriages confer on the male partner undue power over the female partner and any man under the influence of satanic hold will always torture his wife or even kill them eventually.
Below are some of the differences in the mindset of the two concepts.

1. **Traditional**: The woman leaves her father and mother.
   Divine: The man leaves his father and mother.

2. **Traditional:** The man says, "I am your head."
   Divine: The woman says, "You are my head."

3. **Traditional:** The man says, "I am the head of this house."
   Divine: The man says, "Christ is the head of our house."

4. **Traditional**: The man says, "Give me sex, it's my right, if you don't give me I will find another girl who will."
   Divine: Husband and wife seek to pleasure each other sexually and not defraud one another.
   1 Cor. 7: 2-5

5. **Traditional:** The man says, "I'm the one making the money here, I work harder than you do. So I decide how it is spent."
   Divine: Both husband and wife have equal access to the money because her worth and input is beyond monetary value.

6. **Traditional:** The man says, "I'm the one God should speak to concerning family matters and directions."
   Divine: Husband and wife are both joint heirs and God speaks to the woman too in respect of major destiny family direction.

7. **Traditional:** The man "rules" and dominates the woman which is a curse upon the daughters of Eve.
   Divine: The woman submits to the man's love which is a blessing of the daughters of Zion.

3

"It is like feminism has become a license for promiscuity; an excuse for women to cheat like men; act, dress and speak like prostitutes ....It's like coming out of sexual repression from their husbands at home, into sexual oppression in the hands of men on the streets. So what's the point of the feminist gains?"

THE BACKLASH OF THE FEMINIST MOVEMENT

The feminist movement led to significant positive changes in many societies: giving rise to women's suffrage, opportunities to better education, more equitable pay with men, the right to initiate divorce proceedings, the right to make personal decisions regarding pregnancy, protection against workplace discrimination and major legislative victories.

With the passage of the Matrimonial Property Act, an equal division of property upon separation or divorce became a legislation.

As a result of this movement, what is largely not on the radar is the current gender conflict: rise of toxic masculinity and femininity, the erosion of sexual purity, the dampening of relationship excellence and the health of the marital union. Studies reveal that 50% of first marriages end in divorce and 70% of 2nd marriages.

It is common to see changes in economic and social platforms consequently resulting in changes in the society, family and religious structures.

And because the marital and family structures form a very vital foundation of a healthy and functional society, looking away from the following backlashes of the feminist movement can spell disaster for the coming generation.

THE RISE OF TOXIC MASCULINITY

Without character filter such as discipline, self-control and patience, masculine traits like leadership, dominance, combativeness, loudness, aggressiveness, authoritativeness, roughness, crudeness, assertiveness can easily cross into negative territories rife with cruelty, wickedness, abuse, abrasiveness, rashness, uncontrollable behaviors, narcissistic controlling tendencies which can easily make any relationship toxic in a moment.

What is called toxic masculinity is masculine behaviors that can be injurious to a woman's mental, emotional, sexual and physical health; that can lead to emotional disconnection and loss of attraction; that can easily damage a good atmosphere any day.

Toxic masculinity can be abbreviated as good looking men doing well mentally, physically and financially in life but behaving badly in their relationship towards their women. The bad boy syndrome is all about disrespecting, ignoring, denying, mistreating and demeaning a woman in the bid to control her mentally and emotionally, in order to take advantage of her physicality and sexuality without a commitment or price.

As an antidote to the resultant rise of toxic femininity, today's toxic masculinity is working to get the modern women of today to submit and fall in line to male dominance.

The "bad boys" have become very attractive and are getting the chase of many of the beautiful toxic girls out there, and it's like every boy out there wants to be a "bad boy".

We are privileged to mentor a teenager who you would ordinarily think has a boyish mindset but was surprised to learn that all he wanted to be is a "bad boy". What he thought of girls and how he thought they should be treated was just to demean or debase them entirely. Alarmed at this we went straight to spiritual and psychological work!

MEN ARE REFUSING TO GET MARRIED

It is widely believed among younger men of today that the divorce and marital laws especially in the western society are skewed against men. Incentivized by the current divorce laws, 4 out of 5 divorce proceedings are initiated by the female partners, approximate 90% of alimony, 80% of child custody goes to the women.

Research has shown that divorce is harder on men than on women. Generally, men have more to lose in terms of happiness and health after a divorce than their wives. It is commonly reported that weight fluctuations, depression, anxiety, and insomnia are the most frequent health issues men face after going through a divorce.

Struggling with finding ways to cope with identity issues and the added stress that life after divorce brings, men are left vulnerable to high blood pressure, heart disease, and stroke according to studies.
A close relative got divorced recently in the Western society. At the end of the whole saga, he ended up losing half his pension, half of his landed properties, most of which he had bought prior to the marriage due to skewed divorce litigation practices and processes.

Because of stories like this, young men of today are running away from tying the knot. As of 2022, Pew Research Center found, a whopping 63 percent of young adult male in the US want to remain single.
Across Canada marriage is on the decline. The number of marriages registered in 2020 was one-third lower (-33%) than in 2019 (146,121). This happens to be the largest annual decline observed since the vital statistics data on marriages were first compiled in 1921.

Divorce laws which are legislation of Government Intervention became necessary because of the terrible flaws of traditional marriages especially the prevalent abuse and neglect concealed within it.

Why was the divorce law necessary in the first instance? How can you expect a woman who has spent her blood, life, time, energy and sacrificed her career, opportunities out there just to stay home, help you, support you, raise the children, satisfy you etc., go empty handed in case of a divorce?

Introduction of Divorce laws, is however becoming counter-productive because it is encouraging divorce. In the Divine concept of marriage it is unimaginable to conceive divorce because it can be so beautiful and progressive that divorce is the last thing in your mind.

THE RISING TOXIC FEMININITY

Coming out of neglect, emotional abuse and financial subjugation; in search of financial independence; in quest for sexual freedom, power sharing and gender equality; many women have been forced into abandoning their dominant female nature for developing their dormant masculine trait in order to compete with men out there in the market economy. Leaving their traditional role of bread eaters, they have become bread winners too.

To compete and make money in many fields out there among men, today's modern women have become over masculinized.

Just as full masculine men, they have become leaders, dominant, combative, loud, aggressive, authoritative, rough, crude, assertive and also without character filter such as discipline, self-control and patience; such masculine traits will easily cross into negative territories.

Toxic women will destroy any relationship with the stroke of her tongue in a jiffy. They can be as cruel, wicked, abusive, abrasive, rash, uncontrollable, narcissistic, and controlling as men. Sometimes in their craziness, they can break a whole car, beat a man silly, slash tires, become really loud and caustic and in some cases can be worse than men.

In the scripture, men are encouraged to leave their beautiful palace and run to the wilderness just to avoid the toxic woman.

A friend in the ministry, was forced to separate from his wife, against all counsel he declined going back. He said to us, in many years this is the best his blood pressure has been. And he would rather stay single.

Wow! Toxic femininity is women's behavior that can be injurious to mental health and emotional well-being

If being strong, independent and rich as a woman makes a woman attractive to men, why then is it so hard for strong and independent women to find dates nowadays according to recent studies?

May be there is nothing like sexual attraction or seduction by a woman's strength and money.

Masculine men don't really need a woman's money, because functioning in his masculine grace and frame guarantees him success out there and he can make more money.

"Strong and independent" is fast becoming a cover up for female narcissistic tendencies, cut-throat selfish behaviors, proud, egocentric, over masculinized and combative behaviors in today's toxic modern women.

Hating and hurting men, and exploiting rich men by marrying to divorce them down the road, certain modern women have become daughters of hell on the loose, seeking revenge and wanting men to feel the pains their mothers and sisters went through in the past. They have become as narcissistic as toxic men, if not more; fully selfish, now they just don't care anymore.

Oh! How many women today have left their original divine place and role and are now acting out the playbook of Satan, the original displacer and the first enemy of the woman!

"And I will put enmity between thee and the woman, and between thy seed and her seed; it shall bruise thy head, and thou shalt bruise his heel." Gen. 3.15

WOMEN MASCULINIZATION

It is very likely a woman would develop her masculine nature if she grows under an abusive father or a masculine mother or under tough and rough conditions of survival.

Masculine energy is designed for men to dominate and survive in the world. That is what a man needs in the market economy, in war, combat sports, competitive games and business world to have the edge.

A man needs to be ambitious, authoritative, combative, competitive, brave, aggressive, courageous, able to litigate, competent, etc. in order to make success out there in the world.

Modern women today like no other time in history are building their masculine nature at an alarming rate for their own safety, protection and preservation from men and more so, to compete with men out there. Some reject their femininity or dislike being a woman while others envy men's role and would rather be a man or compete with men.

As a result of the 1960 feminist movement, "strong and independent " women have risen up in great numbers, taking on masculine nature, competing with men in many fields out there and abandoning the traditional role of home makers and children raisers.
In exhibiting certain masculine behaviors like aggression, being combative, argumentative, authoritative, she is able to defend herself, make equal money, can afford to live without a man, hence many modern women remain single and are loving their singleness.
However, this is considered toxic femininity, which we believe is the root of the gender conflict prevailing in modern societies today. The gender war is not letting up soon and social media has become the theatre of learning various anti- social behaviors.

We just counseled with a woman who has left her home and husband for many years now. It is very obvious she doesn't want to go back. She's doing better financially, owns her own home, doing much better in her career far much more than when she was married. We asked her how she's coping without sexual intimacy and her new found love with singleness. She retorted, "I'll rather masturbate than return to him" Wow!

SEXUAL EXPLOITATION OF TODAY'S MODERN WOMEN

It is like the Feminist movement stripped some modern women naked, uncovered them and made them targets of demons and men for sexual exploitation.

Having recognized their innate desire for sexual pleasure and liberty from sexual repression, the modern women of today have fully embraced boundary-less sexual escapades tantamount to exploitation by the dark world of toxic sexual masculinity.
Women today have become the primary drivers of open relationships, pornographic world, hot wives phenomena, cuckolding relationships, BDSM, threesomes etc., just to maximize their sexual pleasure.

Many modern women have gone beyond dressing provocatively, exposing the sexual features of their body, into openly engaging in discussions on media shows to boast about their body counts (number of men they have been intimate with).
It is like feminism has become a license for promiscuity; an excuse for women to cheat like men; act, dress and speak like prostitutes.

Reports indicate that over 20% of single women are on anti-depressants, suffering from sexual abuse, molestation, brokenness, wounded, battered and rejected by toxic men.

Modern women are being brain washed to reject and punish the good and nice guys that would treat them well. Like a curse they all want the so called tall, rich, fit and hung below men that would break them.
They spend years chasing after the "bad boys", trying to tame them or seeking to change the 2% of men from cheating on them and they hang in there waiting for the day such boys would stop humiliating and treating them like trash. This is a curse of the daughters of Eve.

"Unto the woman he said, I will greatly multiply thy sorrow and thy conception; in sorrow thou shalt bring forth children; and thy desire shall be to thy husband, and he shall RULE over thee." Genesis 3:16 KJV

The counseling ministry has opened our eyes to the world of women's sexual desire. A beautiful young woman is entangled in a relationship with a toxic masculine man who is extremely verbally abusive to her and is openly reluctant to marry her, but she wouldn't leave him while looking for every way to change him, enduring the pain. She's still at it almost ten years now. And why is she stuck with him? She said the sex is so good! Wow!

In the name of seeking sexual freedom today, research has revealed that 80% of women who pay escorts for sexual rendezvous are married and 40 % of paternity tests in the U.S fail.
Why should sexual liberation be synonymous to sexual promiscuity and looseness?

Having boundary-less sex, roaming the streets looking for the best orgasm is no longer sexual freedom. It's like coming out of sexual repression from their husbands at home, into sexual oppression in the hands of men on the streets. So what's the point of the feminist gains?

In Rebekah's days she said to her husband Isaac, "I'm sick to death of these Hittite women. If Jacob also marries a native Hittite woman, why live?" Gen. 27:46 MSG

I wonder what she would say of the daughters of this world today as a mother of a young man.
As a result of their newly found sexual freedom, modern women today are being heavily sexually exploited by the world of darkness.

Statistics reveal the alarming rate at which women are dissatisfied with their husbands sexually and are seeking divorce for lack of good sex, contrary to the old pattern. They get sexually bored with their husbands very fast; and with the children out of the house and being economically viable to travel the world, they jump ship and go with friends searching for where to get maximum sexual pleasure.

What a temptation out there for modern women today! Who are we to blame for this? Why should our men be so selfish and cruel in exploiting traditional marriage to set up our women this way? Why wouldn't the husbands learn how or make it a duty to pleasure their wives, and make them happy sexually instead of monopolizing the sexual pleasure within the context of traditional marriage concept?

It is becoming alarming that statistics reveal that women now cheat at the same rate as men, and majority of women out of marriage are not seeking to go back to their marriages but would rather seek out young men for maximum pleasure.
Knowing this, many young men out there can't wait to build their manhood and learn the act of turning and tuning a woman's body sexually in order to give her the

maximum sexual experience she is looking for. What an exploitation! What then is the point of the gains of the feminist movement?

Now the few "bulls" (well-endowed men trained in pleasuring a woman sexually), and the few hyper successful predatory men out there are now on a rampage taking full advantage and exploiting today's modern women's sexual freedom.

Can you imagine that she is now the one paying for sex through escort agencies out there, and taking trips across the ocean looking for and paying for that experience?

She has realized, she doesn't need marriage for better sexual pleasure, she doesn't have to cheat on a husband, and she doesn't need a man for money. There are many sites on the internet that can give her all of that. What a sexual state of the modern woman today in the name of women liberation!
Why would she want to go back into traditional marriage? Why wouldn't she be happy divorcing her husband and leaving her home? Wasn't the traditional concept of marriage a total scam to foster the subjugation of women's right including her sexual pleasure?

The bibles says "SURELY oppression maketh a wise man mad…" Eccl. 7:7.

This is like the oppression that women have gone through under men in traditional marriage concept, has led to the current 'madness' of today's modern women!

4

"The true VALUE of a woman is both intrinsically spiritual and physical in nature. Her LOVE is ever transforming. Her WORTH is far more than jewels."

WHO IS A WOMAN ACCORDING TO SCRIPTURE?

Feminism may have opened the eyes of many women to the need to be free from a male dominated society and from the cruel slavery of traditional marital concepts but it is still lacking in potency to make today's modern woman know her true value and worth. What's the point of helping someone to stay away from sugar but not letting them know that energy drinks are worse?

Who is a woman, where did she come from and for what purpose was she made?

SHE IS A DIVINE IDEA.

"And the LORD God said, It is not good that the man should be alone; I will make him an help meet for him." Genesis 2:18 KJV

She is given for man's help. That's why she will always find a man of purpose very attractive.

"For the man is not of the woman: but the woman of the man. Neither was the man created for the woman; but the woman for the man." 1Cor. 11:8-9.

She came from the man, so she has a masculine side to her nature; if and when her natural skills and mind are well developed, she can be a wonder of assistance in many masculine fields.

Every divine idea is loaded with blessings. She is an asset and not a liability, and while her divine role is to help, promote and support the man, her feeding, living or survival is entirely that of the man.

WHAT DOES SHE BRING TO THE TABLE?

A. REST, RELAXATION AND COMFORT

Relaxation exercises decreases heart rate and respiration rate. It lowers blood pressure and increases blood flow. It generally decreases the level of anxiety, depression and insomnia, and mostly relaxes the muscles.

Being emotional by nature, a woman possesses the unique ability to bring a man back into his heart. Relaxing can quieten his mind and make him feel peaceful and calm; and his muscles become less tense and more flexible.

After wandering away in his mind all day, mentally and physically exhausted from the burden, stress, failures and exhaustion of work, war and building, every man needs to relax, refresh, recall, recoil and recoup.
His woman is that perfect machine for his relaxation and comfort.

After war or work, men want to relax. The truckers visit the strip clubs and the C.E.O wants to come home to rest and peace. Women with feminine energy are best suited for masculine rest and balance.
A war general Sisera in Judges 4:17, went into the house of a wrong woman seeking to relax, where he met his demise.
Without relaxation, stress and fatigue will prevail. Stress increases blood pressure and cholesterol, which are major risk factors in the development of heart diseases. Obesity, sexual dysfunctionality, such as impotence and premature ejaculation can also be traced to high levels of stressful activities.

The kings and a lot of hyper successful men out there have found a way to relax in the company of very beautiful ladies, some find the beauty of relaxation in their romantic partners while some other men employ other techniques.
I find it so relaxing whenever my wife massages my neck and the center of my head after a hard day's work, which is usually every day; in no minute I am snoring. I don't know how much I would have had to pay to get that out there. But praise be to God I have found that in a relaxed and restful woman.

I started out driving roughly and carelessly, I got so many speeding tickets and was slammed with high insurance premium. My wife will nag and complain but that didn't get through to me because I felt she had no confidence in my driving and she was always driving the car with me.
This became a very contentious issue in our relationship, especially when we drive together.

Sometimes I try to drive slowly just to avoid the arguments, but that still didn't work until we both realized she needed to rest in the Lord and trust God to drive the vehicle. This was an eye opener for me to the mystery of "Christ is the head of every man"

As soon as my wife found her rest in God, stopped worrying, complaining and nagging, but trusting the Lord, He took over my driving. I can honestly tell you today that it's like Christ took over my driving and I don't speed like that anymore.
Her rest in God introduced rest into my soul. What a mystery! Sometimes we think that we have to worry to change the situation. No, we just have to believe in Christ who is able to change all things in our favor.
A nagging woman opens the atmosphere around her to demonic infestation, but a calm, rested and relaxed woman can easily be a relaxation agent to her man.

While a woman may be able to relax without the presence of a man, studies have revealed that effective relaxation for men often requires the presence of a woman.

Why is this so?
Men are visual beings and a restful and beautiful woman will always be dazzling to his eyes.
Ever since God brought her out of the man and presented her to him in the garden, he has not stopped looking at her till today.

The only thing more beautiful than Lucifer in creation is Eve. That is why Satan is madly jealous of man and would spare nothing to destroy her beauty, using the men. She is also a dazzle to angelic beings and demons. They can't wait to take her over and exploit her sexuality against men.

"For the man is not of the woman: but the woman of the man. Neither was the man created for the woman; but the woman for the man. For this cause ought the woman to have power on her head because of the angels."
1 Cor.11:8-10.

The woman remains a primary target of Satan right from the beginning .The enmity between Satan and the daughters of Eve rages on and can only be won in Christ Jesus.

"And I will put enmity between thee and the woman, and between thy seed and her seed; it shall bruise thy head, and thou shalt bruise his heel." Gen.3:15

God did not give her to demons to use, enjoy and destroy but rather to man for help, pleasure and companionship. God gave her to be protected and taken care of, so God in response can take care of the man. She is a direct link to God who brought her to the man. Her true value is intrinsically spiritual and physical.

But what happens though if a man is clueless or totally oblivious to her true value?
A woman should not be allowed to be under severe stressful situations and conditions as she does not handle stress very well.
Stress appears to be differently experienced between genders: emotional exhaustion prevails in women; while

men tend to feel more depersonalized.
Juggling job pressures, family schedules, money issues, career and educational advancement, and child and elder-care concerns are only a few of the common stressors confronting women today.

Common symptoms of stress in women

Physical: Headaches, difficulty sleeping, tiredness, pain (most commonly in the back and neck), overeating/under eating, skin problems, drug and alcohol misuse, lack of energy, upset stomach, less interest in sex and other things she used to enjoy. (Women and Stress - Cleveland Clinic)

Emotional: Anxiety, depression, anger, unhappiness, irritability, feelings of being out of control, mood swings and frustration.

If you will be needing her for your relaxation later on in the day or in life, then a man must protect her from the stress of coping with the burdens of life.
The assignment to tend the garden, build a good world, family and businesses, and protect them is primarily that of men and was given to man before the woman came on the scene.

The woman may not understand the demand and scope of this assignment, and therefore it may not be her life priority, because the first thing she woke up to in creation is the man and till date the man remains her primary focus. Men do the building and women help.

"And the Lord God took the man, and put him into the Garden of Eden to dress it and to keep it. And the Lord God commanded the man, saying, Of every tree of the garden thou mayest freely eat: " Gen.2:15-16

Men are wired to protect women from the stressful burden of building a good life so she can in turn help him to cope with them. Under heavy pressure and stress, many women break character. Job's wife said, "...curse God and die..." Job 2:9

A woman is best suited to help any man to relax only if she herself is Rested, Relaxed and Calm.
A friendly and smiling woman is an attraction to any man under stress any day.
But what if the real stressor of the woman's life is not the burden of coping with life struggles but the man himself? An immature, toxic man is capable of irrational, erratic, careless, loose, uncontrollable, aggressive and threatening behaviors that can be the root of a woman's deep rooted fears, worries and stressful condition.

A woman must not be left unattended to. Where was Adam when Satan was fellowshipping with Eve in the garden? And how come Lot was unaware that his wife had treasures hidden in Sodom and Gomorrah that made her look back?

Eve was the one deceived. A woman may be vulnerable to demonic attack because of her "emotional" status. A rejected or neglected woman will certainly attract Satan and his minions who can't wait to take over her emotions.

B. HER BLESSINGS

What will the world look like without men? Obviously no world. Our entire infrastructure, the roads, bridges, factories, cars, petrol stations, sewer systems, nuclear plants, houses, coal mines and etc. are pretty much thought up by men, built by men, managed and maintained by men. But how can a man build a home, family, society and a nation without the woman? What value is a product without the people to buy and use it?

A woman's blessings is man-centered. Her blessings are intrinsically more spiritual than physical. If she was meant to be primarily of physical help to a man, wouldn't she have been made as physically strong as men?
So when God said, "It is not good that the man should be alone; I will make him an help meet for him…" he definitely wasn't talking primarily about physical help.

As a man if you're driving on the road and your car gets stuck in a snow bank, who would you rather call for help between a man and a woman passing by? Definitely the man. Of course women are strong and can be stronger than men but not in the physical sphere.

She wasn't created from the raw dust, hence she is certainly not crude or rugged like men. She is a by-product or refined secondary product. She is cleaner and polished. The bible calls her a weaker vessel.
Why then is she being subjected to rigorous labor tasks that she was not designed for in the name of feminism? She doesn't have to be a man to hold her societal value.

If only men would learn to seek God whose idea she was, then will they be able to see her beyond her physical appearance and understand the spiritual dimension of a woman's help.

God had to put Adam under divine anesthesia to bring out the woman, and when he woke up he said this is the bone of my bone, the flesh of my flesh and then called her a woman.
Before the woman, he was engaged fully in naming things and animals. He needed to know her for who she is and see her differently from animals and things. He needed to know that she is as the man but with a feminine side. Every virtuous woman is a blessing to her husband. The bible says she does him well all the days of her life. She is a conduit of joy, peace and rest to her family and to the world around her.

Below are the **Six Spiritual Blessings** a man can access in response to the way he receives and treats her.

1. UNHINDERED PRAYERS: Our prayers are answered according to how we treat our wives. If a man dishonors his wife and fails to treat her with great worth as an heir (partner) in this life, then his prayers will be hindered according to the scriptures. (1Pet.3:7)
Men are working for God as a custodian of this universe and he needs to establish and sustain a link with heaven. Men will always need God to build a better world free of demonic interference and a woman is there to ensure that his divine link remains strong and unhindered. Dishonoring your wife is tantamount to

dishonoring God who gave her to you, and that may be the reason why He doesn't want to hear your voice again.
Can you imagine what your life would look like having your prayers unhindered by any force? And God working with you to build a better world?

2. FAVOR: Abraham became rich because of the king's favor towards Sarah his wife.
God's favor upon a man will open doors of opportunities for greatness and success in life. What if those good things happening to you out there are a result of the gift of that woman you call your wife?

"He who finds a [true] wife finds a good thing and obtains favor from the Lord ". Prov. 18:22

Favour is a highlight of my life and ministry. Sometimes I wonder why some things work to my favor even in the last minute. Treating a wife with dignity and respect can be a world of benefit for your interactions out there in life. So many men go through life on a difficult terrain lacking goodwill. You may want to check in on how you are treating your wife at home.

3. GLORY: The husband of a glorious woman is well respected out there.
"For a man indeed ought not to cover his head, forasmuch as he is the image and glory of God: but the woman is the glory of the man." 1 Cor. 11:7

"Her husband is known in the gates, when he sitteth among the elders of the land." Prov. 31:23

By His grace I can relate to this. I have received honour and glory from places I've never been to, and from men and women I have never met physically just because of who my wife is.

4. ALL ROUND REST, PEACE OF MIND AND GOODNESS: Masculine success cannot buy peace and rest of mind for a man, but a true feminine woman can bring calmness, peace and rest into a man's soul.

"The heart of her husband doth safely trust in her, so that he shall have no need of spoil. She will do him good and not evil all the days of her life..........Her children arise up, and call her blessed; her husband also, and he praiseth her." Prov.31:11-12, 28,

"A foolish son is the calamity of his father: and the contentions of a wife are a continual dropping. House and riches are the inheritance of fathers: and a prudent wife is from the Lord." Prov. 19:13-14

Any environment with good women is always peaceful.

5. LEADERSHIP OPPORTUNITIES/APPROVAL: A man's true leadership quality is revealed by the state of his home.

"Even so must their wives be grave, not slanderers, sober, faithful in all things.
Let the deacons be the husbands of one wife, ruling their children and their own houses well.

For they that have used the office of a deacon well purchase to themselves a good degree, and great boldness in the faith which is in Christ Jesus."
1Tim 3:11-13

You can receive a good degree from home that may open you up to leadership opportunities out there.

6. KEEPING HIM ON TRACK, RESTORER OF PATH:
A true feminine woman has all the potentials to bring a man back from the brink of collapse.

"Likewise, ye wives, be in subjection to your own husbands; that, if any obey not the word, they also may without the word be won by the conversation of the wives; While they behold your chaste conversation coupled with fear." 1Pet. 3:1-2

Oftentimes I hear the voice of reasoning, correction and a mother, like gently bringing a son home, when my wife quietly converses with me on certain issues that is getting out of hand for me.
One day I was being poked very badly to cut relationship with someone but after speaking with my wife, she helped me calculate how much I lost. It was just $60! It was then I realized how satanic that poking was.

In the scripture, Satan provoked David to disobey God. How much I wish it was a chaste woman who spoke to him instead of Joab. David didn't listen to Joab, but in a different scenario, Joab had to fetch a woman to convince David to get his son back from exile. (1Chr.21:1-4; 2Sam.14)

HER WORTH AND VALUE

Adam was busy with work before the woman came on the scene, he was in the business of naming the animals. Adam knew his work before the woman and a man would always go back to his work as a haven but the very first thing that Eve woke up to see was her man. A woman would always run to her man for covering.

To really understand the true value and worth of your woman, a man has to appreciate God who brought her to him which is the main reason why God gives gifts in the first instance. A good wife is a gift that comes with endless possibilities. Prov. 19:14 implies that we can become wealthy and rich through family inheritance, but to get a prudent, congenial, wise, understanding and sensible wife, we have to look to the LORD.

The true VALUE of a woman is both intrinsically spiritual and physical in nature. Her LOVE is ever transforming. Her WORTH is far more than physical jewels.

"An excellent woman [one who is spiritual, capable, intelligent, and virtuous], who is he who can find her? Her VALUE is more precious than jewels and her WORTH is far above rubies or pearls.
The heart of her husband trusts in her [with secure confidence], And he will have no lack of gain. She

comforts, encourages, and does him ONLY GOOD and not evil ALL the days of her life." Prov. 31:10-12 AMP

For today's unregenerate men, she has to bring money and sex to the table before she is worthy of acceptance and love. What a departure from Divine Concept...!! A woman is of far more worth than her looks.

WHAT ABOUT HER INNER APPEARANCE?

Her real dressing is more internal than external. She glows and radiates from within and you can feel and sense her grace and vibes all over the room because she spends more time to dress up from within than without, an attribute that most modern women today easily neglect. Many of them don't even understand how to have their internal dressing in place.

1 Peter 3:1 is not about looking shabby, ugly or unkempt, but rather about consciously putting emphasis on your inner dressing than outward dressing. Naked or shabby within but outwardly gorgeous is of low value and low worth.

"Your adornment must not be merely external — with interweaving and elaborate knotting of the hair, and wearing gold jewelry, or [being superficially preoccupied with] dressing in expensive clothes; but let it be [the inner beauty of] the hidden person of the heart, with the imperishable quality and unfading charm of a gentle and peaceful spirit, [one that is calm and self-controlled, not overanxious, but serene and spiritually mature] which is very precious in the sight of God." 1 Peter 3:3-4 AMP

A woman who is beautiful on the inside can never grow ugly, but old age and condition can change the outward beauty of a woman.
Whenever a woman gets in tune with her true inner feminine nature, she becomes magnetic and shines like diamonds! She is really unstoppable. Kings are looking for her! The moment you are able to see a woman beyond her physical appearance, is the beginning of the unraveling of the treasure of infinite value she brings to the table.
At a point in time my wife had become nonchalant about her outward dressing thinking she was no longer beautiful as she grew older, but the amazing thing was that during this period, I thought she was more beautiful. How come I didn't see her outward appearance though? Because her inner dressing had not changed a bit.

HER PHYSICAL BEAUTY AND ATTRACTION

A woman is a divine specimen and from the day that Adam set his eyes on her, man has not stopped looking. Men are highly visual beings and need help to keep focus on one woman.
It takes a lot of discipline for a man not to look at a beautiful woman and that is why men love to organize and attend beauty pageants.

The queen's beauty was the pride of the king. (Esther 1:11). Abraham knew that Sarah was very beautiful and the men of Egypt would notice her for sure and he was right; even the king Pharaoh saw her. (Gen. 12: 11-15). A woman's beauty is an asset. She cannot be unattractive to her husband. How then is she going to keep and arrest his eyes on her continually?

Enhancing and maintaining a woman's beautiful looks can be trendy and costly. She has to dress in befitting clothes; her skin has to remain smooth and clean; her face, teeth, skin, hair, feet, private areas must remain neat and clean always.

She has to age well. She would be needing dresses for night/bed time, evenings, outings and casual seasons. This may be a financial burden to handle alone without the support of her husband. This must be included in the family expenses to protect her from the enticement of hyper-successful predatory men out there. Home, car and children maintenance should not be a reason to neglect this vital need of a feminine woman.

Her smell, neatness, fitting and elegance will give her the confidence she needs to make her feeling beautiful at all times. Her elegance and fragrance turns men's eyes. Most modern women today want a man who is rich enough to take care of their beauty expenses but the men call them gold diggers. Are they all gold diggers? Yes, some are but some are just concerned about the astronomical expenses of maintaining their beauty. Many women suffering from neglect in this area in their marriage often get rejected by the same man who may

now be looking elsewhere at some other beauty out there just because he has to look. But if you have to look, why not make her the only one to look at by helping her to build her beauty continually.
But if you can respect the covenant of marriage to keep your eyes looking at one woman forever, then you must discipline your eyes by instructing those eyeballs never to look at any other woman other than your wife.

Job said, I made a covenant with my eyes not to look lustfully at a young woman. (Job.31:1)

This is an area that is challenging for most men because there are beautiful women everywhere you look these days.

"Why did you slap me?"….."Why are you looking at her?"……."I'm not looking at nobody"…."Yes you are"….And this argument did not end until they divorced. What a sad end to a marriage just because of a man's weakness not to keep his eyes on his wife. This is the story of one of our counselees. An argument that began from a casual dinner outing

HER SEXUAL HEALTH

We were listening to the YouTube video of a man who recently divorced his wife and his reason was basically because he wasn't getting enough sex.
But on listening closely, when asked what his ex-wife's response to his demands was, he said that she said, "You have to tune me and you're not……" From that point we knew that the divorce was unnecessary. He was not

listening deeply to her heart.

When God was designing sexual pleasure, He had women in mind. Sex did not come into a man's world until the woman was created for him. Science is confirming this and today's modern women are proving it. Traditional concept of marriage confers on men the right to monopolize sexual pleasure, thinking women don't really want it. This is nothing further from the truth.
It was a big error for men to have stolen the value, monopolized the pleasure, and then turn around to shame the woman and repress her through the regimen of culturally tainted traditional marriage. Let us look at some scientific facts that buttress this.

FACTS ON THE TABLE:
1. Women have a greater variety of erogenous zones on her body compared with men.
2. Women have 8000 nerve endings in her clitoris, twice more than that of a man's genitals.
3. Women can experience more, better, longer and different types of orgasmic sexual pleasure than men.
4. Women's sexual drive may increase with age while that of men decreases. 50% of men above age 60 suffer some form of E.D.
5. Women take longer time to reach orgasm and need more foreplay and attention.
6. Women's refractory period is about 2hrs while men ranges from 4 to 20 hours depending on age and health.
7. Women have more health benefits from sexual intimacy than men.

HEALTH BENEFITS OF SEXUAL INTIMACY FOR A WOMAN:

According to Centre for Women's Health, OHSU, below are some of the benefits of good sexual intimacy:
1. Improves brain's health
2. Lowers blood pressure
3. Better immune system
4. Better heart health, possibly including lower risk for heart disease
5. Improved self-esteem
6. Decreased depression and anxiety
7. Increased libido
8. Immediate, natural pain relief
9. Better sleep
10. Overall stress reduction, both physiologically and emotionally

Sex and health are closely linked. In one study, women who reported having a satisfying sexual life had a reduced risk of hypertension. The study's authors posit that the quality of sex is more important for a female's health than the frequency. Having satisfying and happy sex is good for a woman's heart.

SEXUAL FRIGIDITY IN WOMEN
Several studies and research have revealed that many women who are subjected to abuse or put under severe marital stress, such as financial or work stress have reported poor body image, low self-esteem and consequently suffered from sexual frigidity; a condition of unhappiness and disorder that stems from other psychological or emotional pains such as anxiety, depression, fatigue, worry, guilt, fear of painful

intercourse and fear of pregnancy.

It can also develop from the undesirability of a partner, the undesirability of the setting and a desire to get out of the relationship.

Below are common symptoms of frigidity according to National Institute of Health:
1. Decreased sexual desire.
2. Few thoughts related to sex.
3. Less initiation of sexual activity.
4. Decreased sexual excitement or pleasure during sex.
5. Reduced arousal from internal or external sexual cues.
6. Lack of genital sensations during sexual activity.

From the above facts, it is safe to deduce that a well-cared for and superbly nurtured woman, in good health and harmony is sexually healthy and built to enjoy sexual pleasure and must not be objectified, shamed, ridiculed, denied and exploited for it.
Her sexuality must be protected by her husband from sexual predators out there. She does not belong to the streets and demons.

Sexual intimacy must be made more about her than about the man. Traditional marriage on the contrary encourages men to deny her of her innate sexual pleasure and freedom.
But now the feminist movement is turning her into the hands of toxic men and sexual predators who are exploiting, pimping and cashing in on her sexuality while she enjoys it for the most part.

HER FEMININE GRACE

The feminine grace is the balance every true masculine energy needs to survive the onslaught and relentless attack from the darkness of this life.

Her warmth, openness, ability to receive, relax and open things up; her tenderness, softness, quietness and caring nature are so energizing and refreshing to the soul of any man. There is nothing more beautiful than a woman that is fully in tune with her feminine nature.

She receives the seed and nurtures things to birth with her feminine grace. She can incubate the dreams and vision of a man and nurture them to fruition using her feminine power.

In the scriptures, she can be seen as a prophetic custodian of great destinies and making strong decisions which today would have been considered a taboo for a woman in traditional marriage. They had very strong voices!

Sarah: It was 100% her decision to send Abraham's first son away from his father's house, because that was divinely good for them as a family, and God backed her up! Can you imagine that under a traditional concept?

Rebekah: She had a personal relationship with the Lord and understood by divine encounter and revelations who would serve the other concerning the twins within her womb. Isaac her husband had no clue.

"And the children struggled together within her; and she said, If it be so, why am I thus? And she went to enquire of the Lord.
And the Lord said unto her, Two nations are in thy womb, and two manner of people shall be separated from thy bowels; and the one people shall be stronger than the other people; and the elder shall serve the younger." Gen. 25:22-23

Samson's mother: The angel of the Lord did not appear to the husband to reveal the destiny of his son, but it was to his wife he appeared, to download instructions about the life of their son.

"And the angel of the Lord appeared unto the woman, and said unto her, Behold now, thou art barren, and bearest not: but thou shalt conceive, and bear a son. Now therefore beware, I pray thee, and drink not wine nor strong drink, and eat not any unclean thing: For, lo, thou shalt conceive, and bear a son; and no razor shall come on his head: for the child shall be a Nazarite unto God from the womb: and he shall begin to deliver Israel out of the hand of the Philistines." Judges 13:3-5

Mary: Mary was there at Jesus' birth, she was there at every stage till the crucifixion of Jesus Christ. I wonder where Joseph was.

"And the angel said unto her, Fear not, Mary: for thou hast found favour with God.
And, behold, thou shalt conceive in thy womb, and bring forth a son, and shalt call his name Jesus." Luke 1:30-31

Bathsheba: She taught Solomon to be a servant-son and prepared him for the throne. When approaching king David to fight for the destiny of her son Solomon, she called her son a servant in comparison to the other sons of the king. (1 King 1:19)

She taught him prophecy and prepared his heart to be king. By her feminine power she raised and installed a king in Solomon.

"The words of king Lemuel, the prophecy that his mother taught him." Prov. 31:1

Until motherhood fails, no child's destiny can fail. The devil has no chance against the destiny of any child under the custodian of a true mother because of her feminine power.

Hannah: It was Hannah's decision to set up Samuel for his calling. Hannah had such a strong voice at home that her husband allowed her to give their son away to God to serve in the temple. Imagine that happening in the traditional marriage concept.

"For this child I prayed; and the Lord hath given me my petition which I asked of him: Therefore also I have lent him to the Lord; as long as he liveth he shall be lent to the Lord. And he worshipped the Lord there."
1 Sam. 1:27-28

The Shunamite Woman told her husband she perceived a man of God was passing by, and wanted to build him a house, and her husband said go ahead.

Wouldn't that be a difficult conversation in the traditional marriage concept? (2Kings 4:8-10)

Graceful Abigail had access to wicked Nabal's resources and didn't need his permission to do the needful with them. (1Sam.25)

In the chronicles of the kings, the name of the kings' mother is often mentioned. Who and what can a true feminine woman not nurture to life?
A woman in tune with her feminine nature can be super powerful and intoxicatingly attractive.

FEMININE NATURE, FEELINGS AND VIBES:

A woman who has mastered and nurtured her feminine **NATURE** will generate certain positive feminine **FEELINGS** which will radiate or release feminine **VIBES/ENERGY** which in turn is very inviting or attractive to any Masculine male out there.

POSITIVE FEMININE FEELINGS:
Women's feelings are designed to be their communication channel. She says a lot more with her feelings than with her words. What she says some times is not how she really feels, however she is able to truly express her true feelings to a listening ear.

The following positive feelings within a woman depending on intensity are capable of releasing more than enough dose of power or fragrance to change the most difficult or demonic atmosphere in her home and around her man at any time.

1. Feeling Beautiful and Elegant
2. Feeling Magnetic and Inviting
3. Feeling Confident and Affirmed
4. Feeling Desired and Wanted
5. Feeling Capable and Helpful
6. Feeling Safe and Secured
7. Feeling Sexual and Healthy
8. Feeling Special, Honored and Worthy
9. Feeling Cared for and Supported.

A woman through DELIBERATE NURTURING of her feminine NATURE can by herself generate these positive feminine feelings above.

But she may have to contend with many negative factors such as society's anti-women stance, media biases, internet labels/vogue, harsh economic realities, relationship abuse and neglect, poor education, poor parental/ traditional/ cultural backgrounds and religious strongholds.

Not many women are feeling beautiful and elegant enough, not to talk of feeling confident and affirmed in the face of today's bashing of the female gender.

A Masculine father or partner can also easily help to nurture a woman's feminine nature or destroy it. He can help her to feel those positive feminine feelings all the time or most of the time through deliberate intervention that would help her get in tune, focus on or develop her feminine nature.

HOW CAN A MAN HELP?
Through good treatment of giving Compliments,

Validation, Attention, Affirmation, Comfort, Support, Care, Provision, Honor, Protection, Education...etc., her feminine energy would keep rising.

A true masculine partner can make her stay attractive or even more attractive for himself and to other masculine men out there.
But an insecure man, threatened by other masculine men looking at her can do terrible damage to her attraction through Abuse, Caging and Neglect or through deliberate put down and undressing.

The downside of this is that he himself will eventually stop to find her attractive and consequently may start looking at other women out there.

On the lop side, a super attractive feminine woman who is also promiscuous may begin to find the attention from other masculine men irresistible and she may begin to respond to them by flirting or cheating.

WHAT TRAITS MAKE UP THE FEMININE NATURE?

A woman who has come to find rest within her soul and in faith with her God will always release a calming spirit that is not only able to empower the angels to control her atmosphere but will also influence and beautify any atmosphere around her.

By the Spirit of God and help from mentors, a woman can from childhood develop and nurture the following feminine traits within her into a giant nature.

1. Quietness, Sobriety and Meekness 1. Pet.3.3
2. Calm, Relaxed and Comfortable Prov. Prov.21:9, 19
3. Restful and Peaceful. Prov.7:11
4. Warm, Open and Soft. Pro.25:15
5. Birthing and Nurturing. Luke 2:19
6. Accommodating, Welcoming, Hospitable .1Tim.5:10
7. Strong, Healthy and Sexual. 1Cor.7.
8. Receptive and Responsive.
9. Elegant and Cheerful. Esther and Ruth
10. Beautiful. (Appearance and Ambience) Esther, Bathsheba
11. Organizing, Decorative and Creative. Prov. 31
12. Emotional, Emphatic and Trusting: Sarah
13. Submissive, Respectful and Yielding. 1Tim. 2:11
14. Supportive, helpful and serving. Prov. 31.

HER SPIRITUALITY

Rooted in her strong faith, trust and love for her God, she is an embodiment of selfless love who is capable of sustaining her man's destiny on her knees.

Her prayers are born from her deep passion and emotions which enables her to petition, intercede and supplicate in prayers on her husband's behalf, even if she has to endure reproach, denial and delay until she gets her desired response from God. (Math. 21:28)

She is an importunist and because of the nature of her womb, she is not only able to carry and nurture a seed and vision, she is equally capable of bearing a burden until it is dissolved.

She can be so enduring, compassionate and selfless just to see her husband do well and succeed. She is also a true friend and confidant. She is called a virtuous woman.
She is the total opposite of some of today's modern women.

I cannot be more grateful to the LORD for the gift of an Angel given me in my wife. The journey has been tough, rough and bumpy, but thanks for the ever strong spiritual support I am getting constantly through a woman who genuinely loves me.

5

"It is much easier for a feminine woman to recognize masculine traits, focus on them and dish out Appreciation, shower Praises and dress him with Admiration thus popping up his masculine head like a lion."

THE FEMININE WOMAN AND HER MAN

WHY IS HER TRUE VALUE HIDDEN FROM THE NATURAL MAN?

How sad that today's toxic men don't see a woman beyond her sexual value and many damaged women also don't see themselves beyond their physical appearance either.

Why is it hard for a natural ungodly man to fully comprehend the true value and worth of his woman? Why does he always abuse, disrespect or place little value on his woman?

WHY?

He is addicted to his work; he loves and worships his success and income; his worth and value is tied to his earnings. He doesn't need a woman to find work. He was already engaged in the garden before the woman was brought on the scene.

It wasn't him but God that saw the need for a woman, so he doesn't think he needs her. As far as he is concerned, he was working before she came and he was without sexual intimacy before she came! God had to put him to sleep in order to bring her out.

Every man needs to undergo this kind of divine operation and wake up from divine anesthesia to realize she is not a lion or a tiger but the bone of my bone, and the flesh of my flesh.
The unregenerate man with his name calling tendency will label her and call her names that she is not, especially when he is upset.

She is the life of the home, society and nation.

"Every wise woman buildeth her house: but the foolish plucketh it down with her hands."
Prov. 14: 1

A damaged woman will damage everything everywhere. Without value abuse is inevitable.
How can you ever abuse or misuse value if you know it? Everyone is inclined to take care of valuables. This is what is called positive ownership!

People have often wondered why I hold my wife in such high regard and honour. It's because of this truth that dawned on my spirit. I can truly tell you it has made a world of difference in my relationships and my life experiences.

ATTRACTING TRUE MASCULINE MEN

Masculine traits will always attract feminine vibes while a masculine female may have to deal with an underlying repulsion from a masculine male which often results in volatile romantic relationships and communication.

Masculine versus masculine communication failure will result in clashes especially in romantic relationships while feminine to feminine is often boring. Every masculine grace needs its own feminine grace to last or survive in the world. Every masculine male is always seeking his feminine vibes out there or in his own woman in order to reach his balance, rest, calm, peace and stability. All masculine without a feminine grace is the reason why many highly successful men cannot remain at the top of the chain. A masculine man must first be in tune with his feminine nature in order for him to locate or connect that woman with his feminine grace out there. Not all feminine grace out there will suit a man's masculinity. It has to be the type that has its residue or root in the man.

God made man male and female. The woman came out of man and for the man. Her root is in him.

"For the man is not of the woman: but the woman of the man. Neither was the man created for the woman; but the woman for the man." 1 Cor.11:8-9

Toxic masculinity is denying the female nature within a man. All masculinity without a feminine nature is the singular reason why some mighty cruel men, like dictators don't last at the top. One thing common in their fall is that it's usually due to minor or little silly mistakes or omissions.
For lack of balance, an all masculine man will collapse one day due to bad luck or small and unexpected attack. He is not a complete man.

Abraham was a warrior who defeated 4 kings in a battle

with just 300 men but still had enough sense to listen to and honor his wife, and not to get into a fight with Lot his nephew. True masculinity has nothing to do with emotional stoicism, being cruel, abrasive, brash, rude, demeaning, controlling, condescending, abusive and oppressive.

MASCULINE BEHAVIOR IN WOMEN THAT TURNS OFF MASCULINE MEN

The following masculine traits in women attracts feminine men but repulse the masculine men.

1. Combative Aggressive Argumentative, Defensive, Competitive, Assertive, Authoritative.
2. Controlling, Dictating, Taking lead/charge.
3. Insulting, Disrespecting,
4. Mind games, mental control
5. Dislike feminine nature and company...find masculinity offensive...wants to be at par with men.
6. Lack of Empathy.
7. Emotionally stoic, absent, rigid
8. Stubborn and Egotistical
9. Harsh, abrasive, bragging
10. Disrespect for her body and environment.

FEMININITY AND THE SCRIPTURAL LOVE EMOTIONS

"Love endures long and is patient and kind; love never is envious nor boils over with jealousy, is not boastful or vainglorious, does not display itself haughtily.

It is not conceited (arrogant and inflated with pride); It is not rude (unmannerly) and does not act unbecomingly, Love (God's love in us) does not insist on its own rights or its own way, for it is not self-seeking; it is not touchy or fretful or resentful; it takes no account of the evil done to it [it pays no attention to a suffered wrong]. It does not rejoice at injustice and unrighteousness, but rejoices when right and truth prevail. Love bears up under anything and everything that comes, is ever ready to believe the best of every person, its hopes are fadeless under all circumstances, and it endures everything [without weakening]." 1 Cor. 13:4-7 AMPC

Just as most highly masculine men perceive emotional expressions or being vulnerable to a woman as signs of weakness, so are many masculinized women unable to receive loving emotions from men.
Overly masculine female can easily perceive a man's vulnerable kindness as being weak. They may consider being submissive to their husbands as weakness.

A woman by nature is designed to receive love or seed from a man and then birth, reproduce and nurture it back for or to him. The commandment is for the Man to Love his wife as Christ loves the Church. And Jesus loved us first in order for us to be able to love Him back. (Eph.5:28-29, 1 Jn. 4:19)
Most of what is typically being referred to in today's world as feminine nature is what 1 Corinthians 13 describes as love emotions.

A woman in tune with her feminine nature is fully attracted to a man in his masculine grace. She wants him to be in charge but yet gentle and kind. She doesn't mind a warrior with loving hands. She wants him to not only work hard and make money but to also remember to call at break time or bring goodies back home after work.

On the other hand, when a woman is overly masculine, she may find emotional or loving men very repulsive or unattractive. Most of the men that these kind of women would cheat with are men they don't want as husbands. And the ones they want as husbands they call geeks until they are to ready settle down.

The end time plan of Satan is to take men out from the scene and put women in charge knowing he can have his way easily.

"And it was not Adam who was deceived, but [the] woman who was deceived *and* deluded and fell into transgression." 1Tim.2:14

The sinister current of the feminist movement is to emasculate men. Toxic women cannot wait to terminate masculinity. Men are being manhood-shamed like no other time in history.

TODAY'S DECLINING MASCULINITY

Today's declining masculinity in men underscore the effect of poor Parental upbringing, Skewed societal structures, Liberalized Educational system and some lop-sided governing regulations on testosterone development in men.

In today's world, men are becoming more feminized and are being emasculated through the ever changing societal structures.

Society has made certain changes in men's lifestyle that goes against nature. Modern schools, job systems and parental disorders are altering the way boys grow up thus resulting in low testosterone and declining masculinity.

In the past, from the ages of 18 to early 20s boys ritualistically start to take up responsibilities around their house, farm and family business.
They characteristically start building a voice in their communities, providing support for their parents and becoming dependable and reliable, strong young men.

But today's boys make very hard transition into adulthood. They build up a lifestyle that makes it difficult for them to deny self of food, sleep and pleasure.
Many of them are still naive at 18, who know nothing about their world.
They waste their lives eating, partying, smoking, drinking and having sex from high school. And if not that, many waste away getting fat and building bad habits to such a state they become incapable of sacrificing their lust, passion and instant gratification for their future stability and greatness.

Today many boys enter the world not having anything to do or knowing what to do.
Surrounded by a host of entertainment channels that requires little or no effort to access and maintain, they become dependent on others, addicted to pornography and games. It has become normal to waste hours upon hours gaming or watching porn, or on their phones.

Studies reveal that in today's men, testosterone levels are declining and the number of men dating or marrying is significantly down.

The present world emasculating system does not understand that boys by nature cannot just sit around to just learn and do nothing.
He is supposed to be out there engaged in physical activities such as working, gym, farming, sports, exploring, pursuing unique objectives, reaching specific goals and understanding his world.

He has to learn how to EARN, PRODUCE and INVENT. He is supposed to be developing his potentials, building greatness, learning courage, endurance, discipline and mental focus by getting involved in competitive sports, weekly gym exercises which are designed to build his physical body and which in turn will enhance his mental, productive, protective and sexual stamina and strength through testosterone boosting.
Secondly, as a result of the modern women syndrome and the current feminist movement, true masculinity is being eviscerated daily.

The average boy today is intimidated, humiliated and rejected by modern girls as a result of today's women's sexual freedom or liberation and standards.
The very first outcome of the feminist movement from the1960s is the emasculation of true masculinity.
Feminism has become a club of masculine destroyers but incidentally are shooting themselves in the foot.

UNDERSTANDING THE MASCULINE GRACE

According to "Psychology Today", "masculine qualities are clearly adaptive in certain contexts. You need your soldiers to be aggressive (ready to attack and confront), your athletes competitive, and your astronaut stoic."

No culture has ever thrived without a strong contingent of its citizens manifesting masculine traits. Masculine traits are not just needed in the society, they are the makers and keepers of society.
Without men no society can ever function; there will be no world structures, and take out the women there will be no home or family; and without the family structures, what are the world's structures for? Without the consumers what is the use of the producers?

Masculine grace is needed out there in the world of competition, building, combat, sports, mining, and all market economy but to raise a home and build a family, you just cannot treat your wife like your employee.
The beauty of creation is the adaptation and harmony of feminine and masculine grace!

TOXIC MASCULINITY

Being rude cocky, disrespectful, demeaning, volatile, aggressive, dismissive, name calling, bossy, controlling, does not make you an Alpha male.
But getting the home running, business working, children behaving, things moving, being decisive, instructive, focused, hardworking, informative,

firm, tough and strong are what earn a woman's deep respect and submission.

Today's toxic men don't really understand who a woman is and what she is asking for and not wanting to relinquish the dominant superior and oppressive power associated with masculinity, today's men have become far more cruel to modern women.

Toxic masculinity teaches men to deny and reject the feminine nature within them not realizing that feminine nature in a woman came from the man and the root is still there, left there by the Creator so the man can understand her and treat her as equal. (Bone of my bone and Flesh of my flesh)

Toxic masculinity teaches them to confront the masculinized women. Treat them as they would treat men, as equal in the field of masculinity, and give no special treatment; see them lifting something heavy and offer no assistance (after all what a man can do a woman can do right?)

AN INCOMPLETE MAN

Toxic masculinity usually has a bitter end and rife with sudden failure or a snappy fall from the top. Toxic masculinity does not sustain success. And when they would fall, it is usually due to very small mistakes or avoidable traps. Why? Because of lack of feminine grace.

"And Samuel said, As thy sword hath made women childless, so shall thy mother be childless among women.

And Samuel hewed Agag in pieces before the LORD in Gilgal." (1 Sam.15:33)

The king Agag represent the generation of cruel dominant men who love to torture women.

All masculinity without the support of feminine grace will fail in the end. All dictators and cruel bosses without feminine grace have a bitter end in sight. True masculinity is when a man gets in tune with his inner feminine nature to know how to treat and handle his feminine-like personalities out there. As a dominant man, you just cannot be all stoic and unemotional and consequently become incapable of bearing empathic feelings for females or the weak ones out there.

King David was a warrior who never lost a single battle in his lifetime but he had enough goodness within him to still take care of a wounded enemy solder that his cruel master left behind on the battlefield. And it was his kindness to this wounded soldier that led David to the hideout of his cruel master and the consequent destruction that followed.

When David came back from the slaughter of Goliath, it was the women that welcomed him back gallantly with dancing. He must have gone to battle with their goodwill and grace over him.

Jesus our LORD is both the Lion and the Lamb.

All masculinity without the consciousness of the inner feminine nature is what makes an incomplete man. The female came out of the man to make a male.

There is a feminine grace out there for you that is compatible with your inner feminine nature.
Not all female personalities out there will suit your masculinity. It has to be that type of feminine nature that is within you.

CONNECT, MASSAGE AND BUILD HIS MASCULINITY

Masculinity is congruent with masculine feelings developed by building and massaging a man's masculine traits.
To make a man rise to his full masculine frame and cadet, a woman must know how to make him feel Respected, Wanted, Needed, Competent, Courageous, Capable, Strong, Independent, and on Top by working on his masculine traits such as his leadership skills, decision making process, decisiveness, his discipline stance, his bravery, his confidence posture, masculine body pose and fitness, hardworking schedule and mentality, logical and analytical thinking mind set, his dominant nature, his command and communication grace, his physical, mental and sexual strength, and more.
It is much easier for a feminine woman to recognize masculine traits, focus on them and dish out Appreciation, shower Praises and dress him with Admiration thus popping up his masculine head like a lion.
But a toxic woman or over masculinized woman can tear down any man with a stroke of her caustic tongue in a moment.

Making him to feel that you need and want him, and that you believe in him is getting him to think that you are his Angel; that you're uniquely made for him; and he can't live without you.

WAYS TO BUILD AND MASSAGE HIS MASCULINITY.

1. Loyalty and honesty is vital. Never blind side, play games or manipulate him. If at any time you are losing interest in him, talk to him directly and you will be amazed to see how he works hard to gain you back. If you tell a man the absolute truth he feels respected.

2. Never compare him with any other man but ask him to improve for you in areas of your needs that he is lacking or lagging. Most men are motivated to improve to impress their ladies.

3. Give fond care, surprising gifts, present concert tickets, acts of kindness and he will owe you and seek to reward you generously far more than you did; he will think of you as unique, lovely, kind and a mother.

4. Prioritize his vision or demands. If he asks you to do something for him, try to attend to that first before doing anything else if possible and he will feel like your King ready to protect you at all times.

5. Look at him always and give manly compliments. Help him to adjust his tie and outfits if need be and he will think you are his mother.

6. Always occupy a supporting role in his life.

Whenever he wants to engage in a project or program, quickly find a supportive role and make contributions as to how to make it work or happen or better and he will feel he can't do without you.

7. Touch him always. Jump on him, ask him to carry you, walk close by him, and sit close to him always in public settings. Be romantic; being affectionate and romantic will tune him to be conscious of a woman's emotional state. A usually stoic non-romantic man may soon take notice of changes in your feelings and begin to show genuine concern. He has been used to seeing you bubbly and happy.

8. Buy and put on seductive and suggestive dresses just for him and he will feel special. A man's sexual attraction is visual and he will always appreciate beauty and seduction. Seduction makes him think of you sexually.

9. Ask him for help or to do little stuff for you and be super happy/excited that he did it; his light bulb will come on and will want to do more. This is the psychology of favor, which is creating an opportunity for him to show his masculinity, strength and power

10. Attend to him first, greet him first before settling down or before others. Serve him first before others.

Show yourself to him first, he will feel so special and feel like he has to provide for you.

11. Make it easy for him to approach and chase you; be inviting and then withdraw giving him space to plan to chase you. The man in him is like a lion who loves to chase and catch.

12. Respond well to his touches in bed and he will always remember those sounds. They become his music and memorials. He will always want see you again.

13. Ask him for his ideas and opinions, or what shall we do, and celebrate them if they work. He will feel good leading you. Let him suggest the restaurant to take you to, make payment, drive you in your car etc. and he will always want to be your man.

14. Adore his masculine features: tool, biceps, thighs, swag, fitness, physique, height, chest, upper body, and he will always want to see you. Men hardly gravitate towards any woman that would reject their masculinity.

15. Be positive, soft and romantic. Focus more on having fun with him.

16. Suggest new activities to create memories and bonds.

17. Keep yourself busy. Never revolve your life around him. Give him space when necessary but never prolong it and always look forward to re-connecting him with glee.

18. Give him an endearing macho name that suggests he

is strong and powerful and he will always want to perform for you. Music artists arouse you to the dance floor by singing your praises. Master how to arouse him. Every man is unique and different.

ABIGAIL AND THE FOOL

Having said all, not all men or women are toxic but a few can be really foolish. Counselling with a young woman who is separated from her husband and seeking to get out of her marriage; in response, she said, "My husband is not really toxic, he can be a good man when he wants to be, but I have never seen a man that can be as foolish as him...."

She went on to reiterate how trying to get him out of debt is liking pulling teeth, as soon as one is paid off he is back at it again for the most unreasonable expenses; no plans for the day not to talk of the future; wasting valuable time and resources; getting in and out of trouble just because of association with slackers as friends. She has lost all attraction for him, all connections are broken, and she just cannot communicate with him in any sensible manner. She wants out and never to go back.
In less than a year of separation from him, she has completed a college course program, improved her credit score by 150 points, got herself out of debt and doing well mentally and physically.
Wow! This one is a challenging nut to crack!! Even Abigail a super feminine in the scripture could not change "foolish Nabal" of the bible.

OUR MISSION

Together, we can limit the influence of toxic femininity and masculinity over our youths and relationships; raise the King's daughter in our women and raise the husband in Christ in our men; heal hurting relationships by restoring marriage after the order of divine concept and break the hold of the traditional concept.
This book lays the foundation of knowledge to get this done.

ABOUT THE AUTHORS

Rev Olu and Vicki David have been friends since 1982 and married since 1988 with over 40 years of relationship excellence.
Their marriage is an offshoot of the throne room of love and power.
With their expertise in connection, communication and emotional management they have helped hundreds of couples and counting to address various issues in relationships, including regaining lost connections, developing romantic gestures to revive relationships, healings from trauma and abuse, addressing abusive tendencies and mentoring many more in relationship management.
The Lord recently released them to deliver this wealth of wisdom to stem the ugly tide of toxic masculinity and femininity and restore relationship wholeness
through termination of the work of Connection killers, Communication destroyers and Emotional blockages in romantic relationships thus giving no room to marriage/relationship destroyers.

FOLLOW US:
YOUTUBE, FACEBOOK and INSTAGRAM
Revealed Word Broadcast

- For Prayers/ Marital Counseling Needs, you can Call, Text or WhatsApp. **+1 905 767 0925/+1 905 720 0909/+1 705 426 7353**

- To Share your Praise Reports/Testimonies, Text or WhatsApp to **+1 905 242 7818**

Made in the USA
Columbia, SC
16 July 2023